MW01056962

MY LIFE TURNED UPSIDE DOWN, BUT I TURNED IT RIGHTSIDE UP
By Mary Blitzer Field and Hennie Shore
Illustrated by Bruce Van Patter
Self-Esteem Series Editor: Hennie Shore
Art Director: Charles D. Brenna
Design: Christopher Laughlin

© 1994 Childswork/Childsplay, LLC, a subsidiary of Genesis Direct, Inc.,
100 Plaza Drive, Secaucus, NJ 07094.   All rights reserved.
For questions or comments, call 1-800-962-1141.

Childswork/Childsplay is a catalog of products and publisher of resources for mental health
professionals, teachers, and parents who wish to help children with their social and emotional growth.

No part of this book may be reproduced or transmitted in any form or by any means, electronic or
mechanical, including photocopying, recording, or by any information storage and retrieval system
without written consent from the publisher.

ISBN 1-882732-06-5

Other products by Childswork/Childsplay:

Play-and-Read Series Books
ALL ABOUT DIVORCE
ALL FEELINGS ARE OK–IT'S WHAT YOU DO WITH THEM THAT COUNTS
FACE YOUR FEELINGS
EVERY TIME I BLOW MY TOP I LOSE MY HEAD

Self-Esteem Series Books
SOMETIMES I DRIVE MY MOM CRAZY, BUT I KNOW SHE'S CRAZY ABOUT ME:
   A Self-Esteem Book for ADHD Children
THE BUILDING BLOCKS OF SELF-ESTEEM: A Skill-Oriented Approach to Teaching Self-Worth
EVERYTHING I DO YOU BLAME ON ME!: A Self-Esteem Book to Help Children Control Their Anger

Reference Books
THE BOOK OF PSYCHOTHERAPEUTIC GAMES

Psychological Games

THE ANGRY MONSTER MACHINE	KIDS IN COURT
THE CLASSROOM BEHAVIOR GAME	LOOK BEFORE YOU LEAP
THE DINOSAUR'S JOURNEY TO HIGH SELF-ESTEEM	MY TWO HOMES
DR. GARDNER'S PICK-AND-TELL GAMES	STOP, RELAX & THINK
THE GOOD BEHAVIOR GAME	YOU & ME: A GAME OF SOCIAL SKILLS
THE GREAT FEELINGS CHASE	

For a free catalogue of books, games and toys to help children, call 1-800-962-1141.

MY LIFE TURNED UPSIDE DOWN, BUT I TURNED IT RIGHTSIDE UP

A Self-Esteem Book About Dealing with Shared Custody

By Mary Blitzer Field and Hennie Shore

Illustrated by Bruce Van Patter

Childswork Childsplay

Secaucus, New Jersey

For Parents

Shared custody can be one of the most difficult challenges that parents may encounter. Everyone wants what is in the best interest of the children, but the emotions and needs of the parents may sometimes get in the way.

Ultimately, however, children must develop their own coping mechanisms to make a realistic adjustment to the change. This book was written to give children ways that they can cope with this "unasked for" time in their lives.

This may be the first "upside down" book you've ever read. When you read it, the arrows will point you in the right direction. When you come to a page that is upside down, turn the book over and continue reading. Every other page will require you to turn the book as it offers practical solutions to the problems that may arise when parents divorce and decide on shared custody. In addition to holding the interest of children, the action of turning the book upside down will help them realize that they can take charge of the problems that occur in their lives and find practical solutions that will help them feel "grounded" again. Children can learn that they indeed can turn their lives rightside up.

We hope that you will take the time to read this book with your child(ren), and that it will give your family an opportunity to address the individual issues that are special to your situation. The more parents make themselves available for discussion, whenever the moment arises and wherever the conversation might lead, the better children will be able to accept the changes that come with divorce. We have also included several worksheets in the back of the book which you can copy to help your child keep track of important places, things, and events.

It is important to recognize that the first year following a physical separation is the most critical time in the overall adjustment of children to divorce. Often, their lives truly do "turn upside down." Their feelings concerning divorce later in life will bear directly on the early opportunities they have had to talk about their own experiences.

For Children

This is a fun book, but it also has a message. On the first pages, the girl in the book begins to tell us the problems she had when her living situation changed because of her parents' divorce. Then, on the next page, you have to follow the arrow and turn the book upside down to find out how she solved her problem. That's how the whole book goes.

Maybe you feel that your parents' separation or divorce turned your life upside down, too. But you can make things better. Not all at once, but one problem at a time. We hope that this book will give you some new ideas to help turn your life rightside up.

This is a "solutions" book. That means that I had some problems, but I found out how to solve them.

When my parents got divorced last summer, I felt like my whole world had turned upside down. But step-by-step, I turned things rightside up. This book tells how.

Sometimes it's hard for me because my parents live in two different places.

When I was at Mom's, the toys I wanted to play with were at Dad's house. When I was at Dad's, my favorite toys were at Mom's...

4

So I made a list of all my favorite things and decided which to leave at Mom's and which should stay at Dad's.

Make lists to help keep things organized.

5

I missed my Dad so much when I was at Mom's...

But he said I could call him at his office or his apartment whenever I wanted to, and I put a picture of him in my locket.

Find special ways to keep in touch with a parent who moves away.

7

I was afraid to get angry at Mom because I thought she might leave me too. My stomach hurt all the time...

But I decided to take a chance and tell Mom how I felt, and my stomach aches went away.

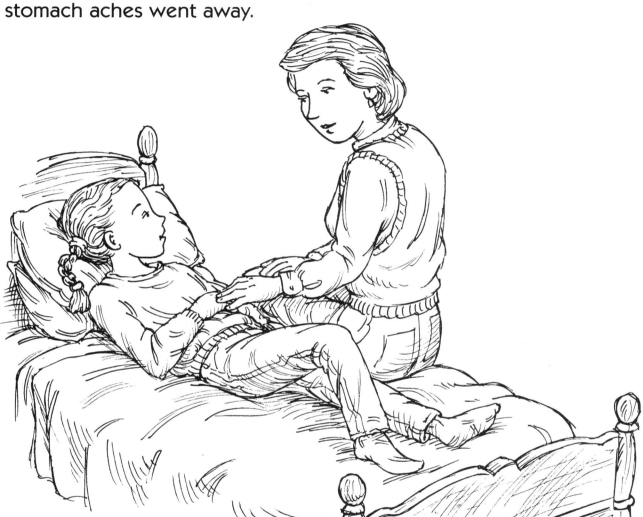

Talk to your parents about how you feel. It helps!

At first, Mom didn't spend much time with me. It seemed like she cried all the time...

So I said, "I need your help, Mom," and she started to pay more attention to me.

Ask for help when you need it.

In the beginning I felt like I didn't have any privacy at Dad's because his apartment was so small...

So we strung up some pretty sheets on a clothesline, and now I have my own private place.

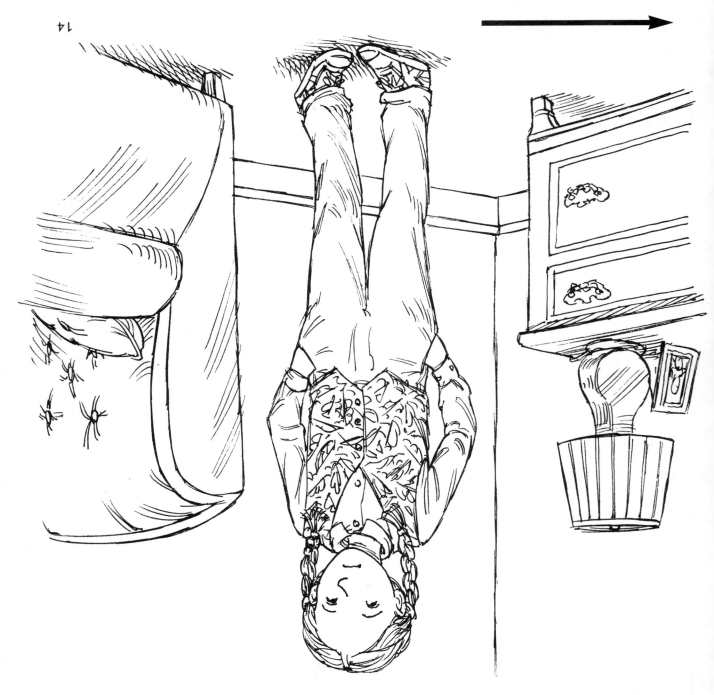

I also didn't feel "at home" at Dad's new place...

But Dad let me pick out some stuff for my new room, and I put some cool posters on the wall. It wasn't long before my new room looked great!

If you feel uncomfortable in your "second" home, ask for your own special space.

Mom got angry when she thought Dad was buying me too much stuff that I didn't need...

But I told her that she should talk to Dad about it, not me, so she did.

When your parents get angry at each other, ask them to leave you out of it.

17

My friends were so far away when I was at Dad's. I was worried that I wouldn't be able to see them...

But Dad would drive me to a friend's house, or sometimes a friend would come to play at Dad's.

Tell your parents when you want to spend time with a friend.

Sometimes Mom didn't want me to call Dad when I was with her...

But I told her that I needed to talk to him, because I missed him, and she said, "Okay."

It's always okay to tell one parent when you miss the other. Parents understand that you love them *both*.

Whenever I'd go to Dad's he'd want to know everything I talked about with Mom...

And I told him that some things are private, just between Mom and me.

It's all right to keep some things to yourself.

And I really hated when Mom and Dad would say bad stuff about each other to me...

I told them that I didn't want to be "in the middle," and they stopped doing that.

Ask your parents to be fair by keeping their angry comments to themselves.

25

I had trouble concentrating at school because I wished things could be like before the divorce...

I talked to the school counselor about it, and now I feel much better.

When you're having a problem, talking about it can help.

Sometimes I got mad at Dad when he was late picking me up...

So Dad and I got matching watches and Dad said he'd pay more attention to the time.

When you're mad about something, ask your parents to help you with a solution.

One time Dad had to go on a business trip when I was supposed to stay with him for the weekend...

I stayed with Mom instead and when Dad got home we went out for pizza and a movie.

When a visit must be cancelled, it's okay...just try to make the next visit *extra* special.

I didn't think it was fair that I had to make my bed at Dad's—after all, I wasn't there that much...

Dad said now that I lived in two homes I had responsibilities in both places, and that making my bed was my job. Now I make my bed every day wherever I am, and Mom and Dad both say I do a great job.

Having two homes means being a helpful family member at *both* places.

Once when I was at Dad's I left my book report at Mom's, and it was due the next day!

Now I have a homework folder that is always in my backpack, whether I'm staying with Mom or Dad.

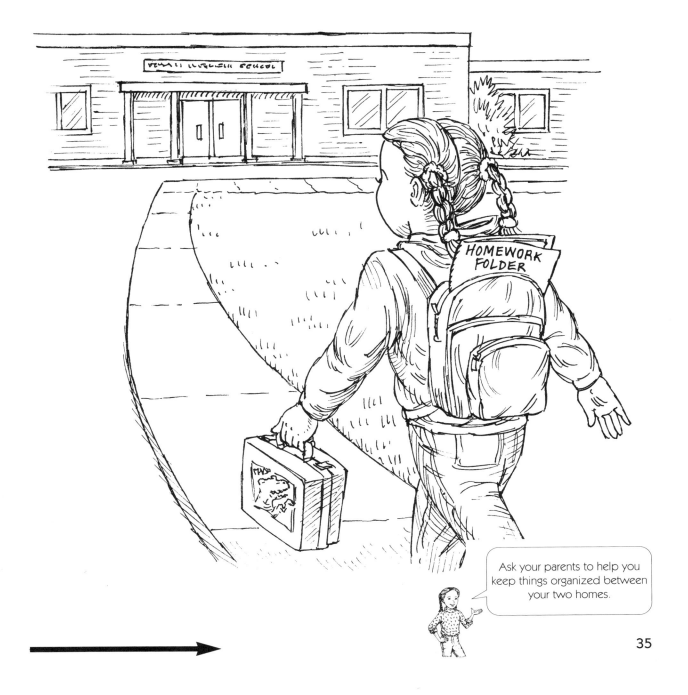

One Monday at school my friend Kate said, "Why didn't you come to my birthday party yesterday?" I felt awful, and I said, "Oh, Dad forgot."

So that evening we made a special calendar that I could take to both houses. We marked different activities in different colors, and I wrote in all the important stuff.

Making calendars or "to do" lists will help you remember important events.

I hated when Mom went out on dates...

But she told me that she needed to do things on her own, like go out on dates, but that didn't mean she loved me less.

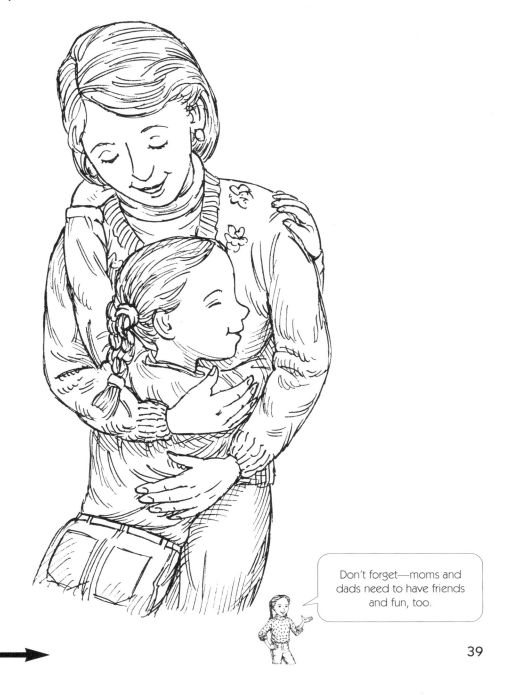

Don't forget—moms and dads need to have friends and fun, too.

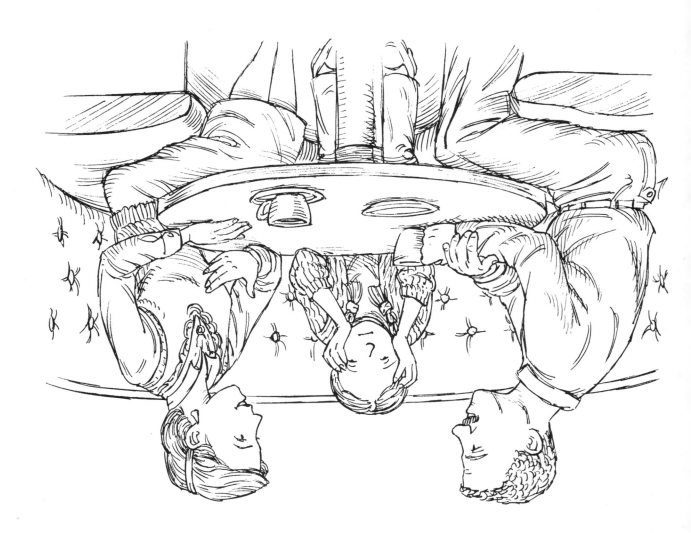

Once Mom even took me on her date with Chuck and they ignored me the whole time...

I told Mom how much I hated that and the next week we all went bowling. We had a great time!

Tell your parent if you're feeling left out.

For a while, it seemed like Dad was dating every woman he met, and I guess I was mean to them...

He saw that I was upset and said he would only have me meet the ones he really liked.

Tell your parent if you think he or she is not thinking of your feelings.

43

Sometimes I think terrible things about both Mom and Dad because I get angry at them for getting divorced...

The school counselor told me that just because I get mad doesn't mean I'm a bad person, and that it's okay to feel anything.

"Bad" feelings are okay... everyone gets mad sometimes.

At the beginning of the school year I was afraid that the other kids would think I was weird because I had two addresses...

But when my teacher sent the class list home, I saw that **a lot of** the kids live in two homes.

47

Dad and I went on so many weekend trips that I started to wish we could just stay home and "hang out..."

So I asked him if we could, and he said, "Great idea!"

When all you want to do is just "be together," express your feelings.

For a while it felt like Mom wanted me to clean up all the time...

She said, "I need you to do more around the house," so we made a job chart and now it feels like things are fair.

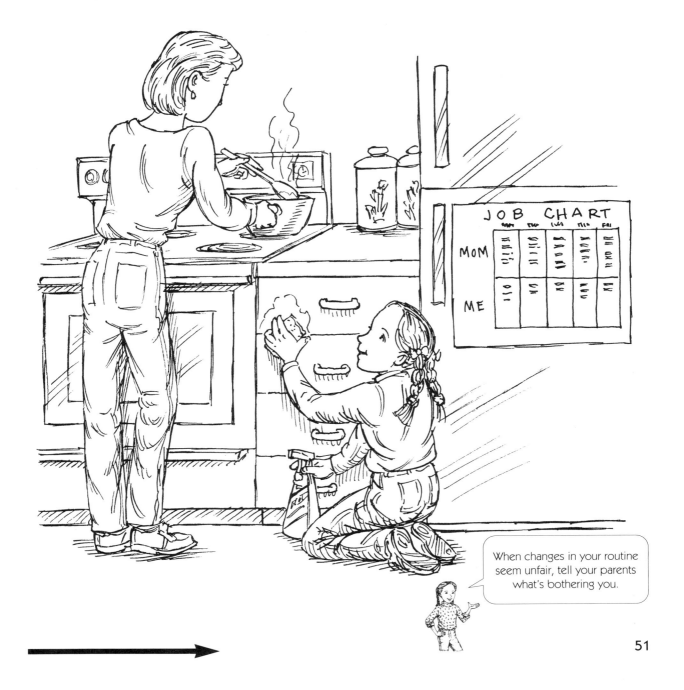

When soccer season started Mom said she didn't have to come to my games when Dad was there...

But I really wanted both of them to come, and she saw how much it meant to me when she came.

Parents aren't 'mind readers.' When you need both of your parents to be there for you, tell them.

Sometimes I'd be at Dad's and he'd seem really sad and quiet...

He told me he was going to see a therapist to help him feel better, like the counselor I talk to at school.

Just like kids, parents can also feel better by talking about their feelings.

I was worried about leaving Mom alone at Christmastime...

I called her from Dad's to see how she was and she sounded okay. She told me not to worry about her and to have a good time, so I did.

When your parents tell you they're fine, believe them and stop worrying!

When I came home from my vacation with Dad I couldn't wait to see Mom. But Chuck was there and I felt like he'd taken my place...

I told Mom I wanted to be with her alone, so she said, "From now on, we'll have some 'special' time together every day— just us."

If you want to spend more time alone with your mom or dad, express yourself.

I like Chuck, but the first time he slept over I was so mad...

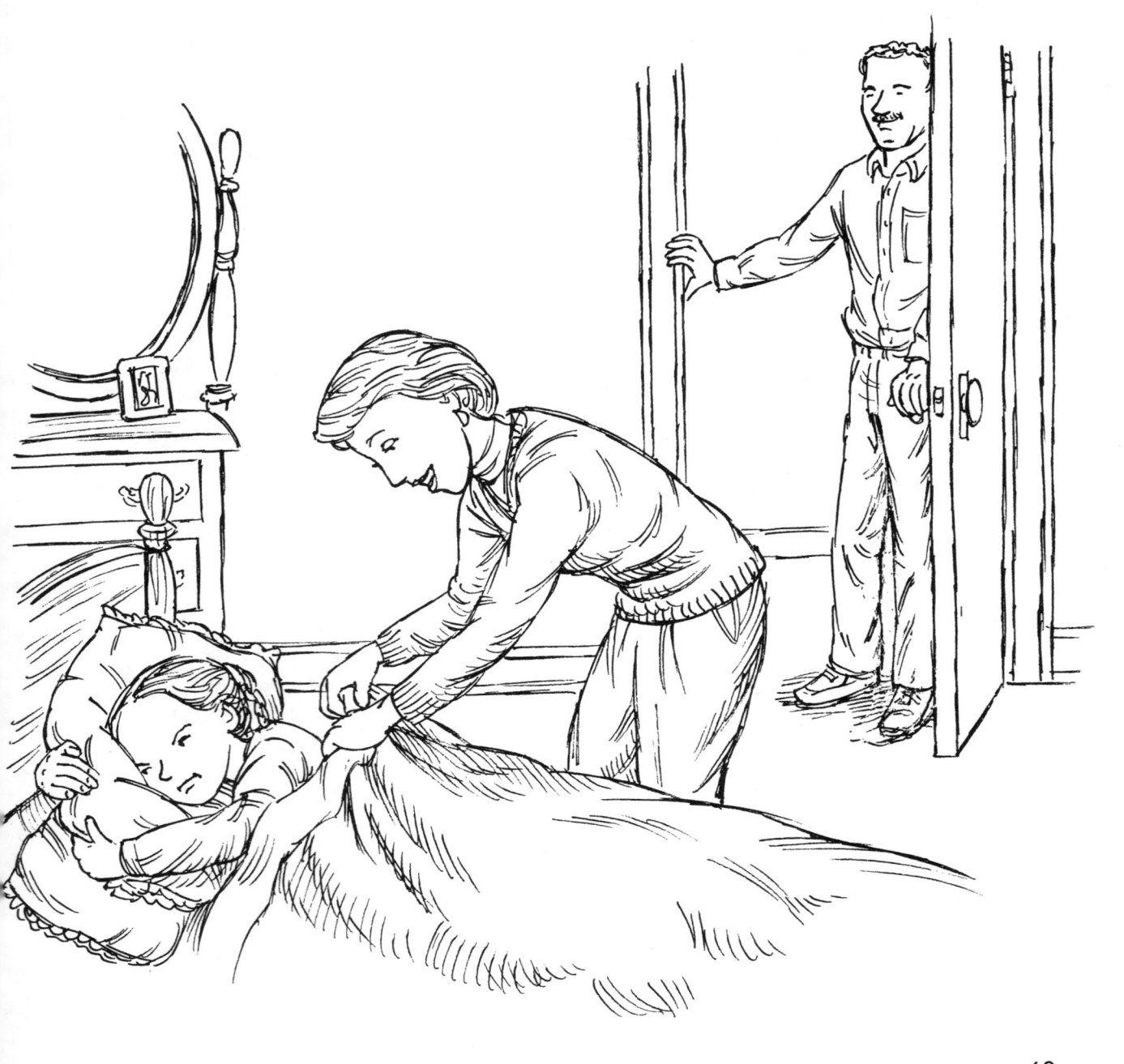

But he was funny at breakfast when he spilled his juice and after a while I liked having him there.

Getting to know the special people in your parents' lives can be fun.

One day in spring Mom told me that I couldn't see Dad anymore until he sent the money he was supposed to send...

She told me that the lawyers and Dad would have to work it out, and that I could talk to Dad on the phone. It took a little while but they worked it out.

I used to think that if I did everything Mom and Dad wanted me to do all the time, they would get back together...

But I realized that the divorce had nothing to do with me, and that they are both happier now.

Divorce is never a child's fault, so don't blame yourself.

Mom, Dad and I have all been through a lot of changes, but I've learned that new things don't have to be bad, and that problems can be solved. When your life turns upside down, you can turn it rightside up.

FORMS TO HELP YOU GET ORGANIZED

SPECIAL EVENTS CALENDAR

Use this Special Events Calendar to help you organize the important events of each month. Copy this sheet and then fill in the days of the month. Circle "At Mom's" or "At Dad's" so you know where you'll be staying on each date.

MONTH: _____

	SUN	MON	TUES	WED	THURS	FRI	SAT
WEEK OF _____	AT DAD'S / AT MOM'S	AT DAD'S / AT MOM'S	AT DAD'S / AT MOM'S	AT DAD'S / AT MOM'S	AT DAD'S / AT MOM'S	AT DAD'S / AT MOM'S	AT DAD'S / AT MOM'S
WEEK OF _____	AT DAD'S / AT MOM'S	AT DAD'S / AT MOM'S	AT DAD'S / AT MOM'S	AT DAD'S / AT MOM'S	AT DAD'S / AT MOM'S	AT DAD'S / AT MOM'S	AT DAD'S / AT MOM'S
WEEK OF _____	AT DAD'S / AT MOM'S	AT DAD'S / AT MOM'S	AT DAD'S / AT MOM'S	AT DAD'S / AT MOM'S	AT DAD'S / AT MOM'S	AT DAD'S / AT MOM'S	AT DAD'S / AT MOM'S
WEEK OF _____	AT DAD'S / AT MOM'S	AT DAD'S / AT MOM'S	AT DAD'S / AT MOM'S	AT DAD'S / AT MOM'S	AT DAD'S / AT MOM'S	AT DAD'S / AT MOM'S	AT DAD'S / AT MOM'S
WEEK OF _____	AT DAD'S / AT MOM'S	AT DAD'S / AT MOM'S	AT DAD'S / AT MOM'S	AT DAD'S / AT MOM'S	AT DAD'S / AT MOM'S	AT DAD'S / AT MOM'S	AT DAD'S / AT MOM'S

NAMES AND NUMBERS SHEET

Copy this Names and Numbers sheet so that you can leave one at Mom's and the other at Dad's.

NAMES	PHONE NUMBERS

HOMEWORK HELPER SHEET

This Homework Helper sheet will help you to remember when long-term projects are due. Copy this sheet and then fill in the days of the month. Circle "At Mom's" or "At Dad's" so you know where you'll be on each date. If you have a spelling test coming up, write it in, or a book report due, write that in, too. Write in anything that will help you remember when assignments are due.

MONTH: _____

MON	TUES	WED	THURS	FRI
AT DAD'S AT MOM'S	AT DAD'S AT MOM'S	AT DAD'S AT MOM'S	AT DAD'S AT MOM'S	AT DAD'S AT MOM'S
AT DAD'S AT MOM'S	AT DAD'S AT MOM'S	AT DAD'S AT MOM'S	AT DAD'S AT MOM'S	AT DAD'S AT MOM'S
AT DAD'S AT MOM'S	AT DAD'S AT MOM'S	AT DAD'S AT MOM'S	AT DAD'S AT MOM'S	AT DAD'S AT MOM'S
AT DAD'S AT MOM'S	AT DAD'S AT MOM'S	AT DAD'S AT MOM'S	AT DAD'S AT MOM'S	AT DAD'S AT MOM'S

About the Authors:
Mary Blitzer Field holds an MA in English Literature from Columbia University and teaches writing and literature at Villanova University. Currently residing near Philadelphia, she is the author of All About Divorce *and writes for a variety of medical and psychological publications. The daughter of a psychoanalyst, the wife of a psychologist and the mother of two school-aged children, she brings a special perspective to bear on topics relating to child psychology.*

A long-time editor and writer for various trade and consumer magazines and periodicals, Hennie Shore is Senior Editor for The Child Therapy News *and author of* The Therapist's Toolbox: Vols. I and II. *She resides in Wynnewood, Pennsylvania with her husband and two children.*

About the Illustrator:
Bruce Van Patter has worked as a children's book, magazine and textbook illustrator for 13 years. He lives in Phoenixville, Pennsylvania with his wife and three sons.

About the Self-Esteem Series:
Self-esteem is more than just liking oneself. It is a deep and overriding sense of self-worth and well-being, which comes from a realistic sense of competency and success in the world. The Self-Esteem Series addresses the challenges of children who may feel "different" and offers solutions in helping them develop a positive self-image.